WHAT A LOAD OF BALLS

Over 200 ball sports facts

ALF ALDERSON

DOG 'n' BONE

First published in 2016 as *Ball Sport Trivia*
This edition published in 2018 by Dog 'n' Bone Books
An imprint of Ryland Peters & Small Ltd

20–21 Jockey's Fields   341 E 116th St
London WC1R 4BW   New York, NY 10029

www.rylandpeters.com

10 9 8 7 6 5 4 3 2 1

Text © Alf Alderson 2018
Design and illustration © Dog 'n' Bone Books 2018

A CIP catalog record for this book is available from
the Library of Congress and the British Library.

ISBN: 978 1 911026 61 7

Printed in China

Editor: Marion Paull
Designer: Jerry Goldie
Cover design: Eliana Holder
Illustrator: Blair Frame

CONTENTS

FOOTBALL

> "The word 'genius' isn't applicable in football. A genius is a guy like Norman Einstein."

JOE THEISMANN Sports analyst and former NFL quarterback

ODD BALLS

In the 1905 season, 19 players were killed and 150 seriously injured. President Theodore Roosevelt threatened to close the game down unless it was made safer.

According to declassified CIA records, Adolf Hitler's rallying cry "Sieg Heil!", meaning "Hail Victory", was modeled on the techniques used by football cheerleaders.

Twelve new footballs, sealed in a special box and shipped by the manufacturer, are opened in the officials' locker room two hours prior to the start of an NFL game. These balls are marked with the letter "K" and used exclusively for kicking.

It takes about 3,000 cows to supply enough leather for a year's worth of footballs used by the NFL.

If you applied for a
Green Bay Packers' season ticket
today, you'd have to wait almost
1,000 years before
receiving one.

Since 1941, the official supplier of balls
to the NFL has been Wilson, the world's
biggest manufacturer of footballs.

Wilson produce some 4,000 balls per day, many by
hand. Their Duke model has been used in every
NFL game for 75 years.

According to a study in *The Wall Street
Journal*, a standard NFL game on
TV features just 10 minutes and 43
seconds of action, while commercials
account for another 60 minutes or so of
the three-hour game.

**The average lifespan for an NFL player in 1994
was 55 years compared with 77.6 years for the
rest of the US population.**

During the 1958 NFL Championship game, a National Broadcasting Company (NBC) employee ran onto the field, posing as a fan, in order to delay the game, because the national television feed went dead.

MOB RULE

In Jamestown, Virginia, "football" games in the early seventeenth century were similar to the various mob football games played in Britain, using a rudimentary ball made from an inflated pig's bladder.

In the early nineteenth century, students in universities such as Yale, Harvard, Princeton, and Dartmouth played with a ball similar to a British rugby ball. These games were spectacularly violent—so much so that Yale and Harvard banned them for a time in the 1860s.

In 1876 a set of rules was drawn up based on those of rugby union, and the Intercollegiate Football Association was formed. In the 1880s Walter Camp, the "father of American football" introduced various new rules that differentiated the game from rugby.

GET A GRIP

By the mid-nineteenth century, balls were being manufactured in a consistent shape, which made both kicking and handling easier.

In 1934 the circumference of the ball was set at its current size in order to make it easier to grip and throw, but other than improvements in the actual manufacturing process, the way a football is made has changed relatively little in decades.

NFL football fields must be built facing north/south or in the shade, so that the sun doesn't interfere with play.

"You have to play this game like somebody just hit your mother with a two-by-four."

DAN BIRDWELL former NFL player

> "Most football players are temperamental. That's 90 percent temper and 10 percent mental."

DOUG PLANK NFL football coach

WHAT'S BROWN AND STICKY AND COMES FROM COWS?

The best footballs are made from brown, tanned cowhide with various forms of weatherproofing and a "pebble grip" texture or tanning to provide a tacky grip.

The white stripes at either end of the ball are designed to improve grip. On top-quality balls they are stitched on rather than painted.

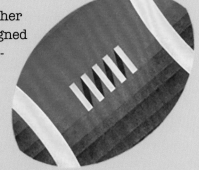

NFL players have been
fined up to $5,000 for
giving a game ball
to a fan.

BALL CONSTRUCTION

In terms of construction, a football consists of four
panels that are stitched together, two of them
being perforated along adjoining edges to allow for
lacing. One of these two panels has an additional,
reinforced perforation to hold the ball's inflation
valve. An interior, multi-layer lining is attached to
each panel to provide better shape and durability,
and the panels are stitched together inside out,
leaving the lacing hole, through which the panels
are pushed after stitching to turn the ball right-side
out. A three-ply polyurethane bladder is inserted
through the lacing hole to improve air retention and
moisture control.

The last process is inserting the laces, which are
important for obtaining a good grip when holding
and throwing, and may be made of leather or
polyvinyl chloride (PVC).

HARDER, BETTER,
FASTER, LONGER

The tackles regularly taken by football players are some of the hardest in sport. A study by Virginia Tech revealed that players regularly receive hits of over 100Gs, sometimes reaching 150Gs—more than enough to knock the ball out of a player's hand. To give you a comparative force, a slap on the back is usually around 4Gs.

In 1940, the Chicago Bears beat the Washington Redskins 73–0, recording the biggest ever winning margin in an NFL game. The Redskins restored some pride 16 years later, when they defeated the New York Giants 72–41 in the highest scoring NFL game of all time.

The fastest NFL player ever to take to the football field was Dallas Cowboys wide receiver Robert "Bullet Bob" Hayes. Not only did he dominate on the field but also on the track, where he won the 100 meters at the 1964 Summer Olympics, setting a new world record of 10.06 seconds in the process.

The longest successful field goal in an NFL game is by Matt Prater of the Denver Broncos, who hoofed the ball 64 yards. In 2015 a video surfaced of a Texas Longhorns practice session, where kicker Nick Rose made an 80-yard field goal look easy.

2

BASKETBALL

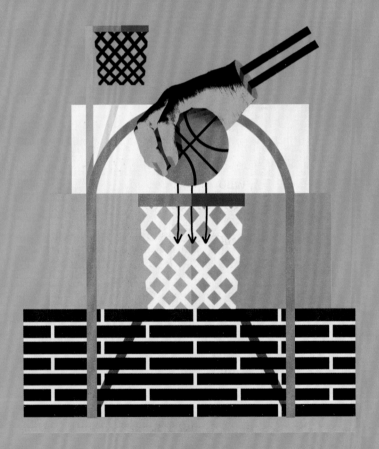

> "I'm tired of hearing about money, money, money, money, money. I just want to play the game, drink Pepsi, wear Reebok."

SHAQUILLE O'NEAL
Former NBA pro turned TV pundit

ODD BALLS

The smallest ever NBA (National Basketball Association) player was Muggsy Bogues at 5ft 3in, who played for the Washington Bullets in the 1980s.

The tallest was Romania's Gheorghe Mureșan at 7ft 7in, who also played for the Washington Bullets but in the 1990s.

Detroit Pistons' Isiah Thomas scored 16 points in 94 seconds against the New York Knicks in the 1984 NBA playoffs to force the game into overtime— and his team still lost.

The first professional basketball game was played in Toronto, Canada in 1946.

In 1992, two legendary MJs, Michaels Jackson and Jordan, appeared together in the music video for the King of Pop's single, *Jam*. A basketball that featured in the video was signed by the pair and in 2010 was auctioned for a staggering $294,000. Jordan-related memorabilia is in high demand. In 1992, McDonalds released a limited-edition burger imaginatively titled the McJordan. A bottle of McJordan BBQ sauce was sold at auction for $9,995, 20 years later.

Early basketballs were brown.
Orange balls appeared in the 1950s and orange is still the official color for NBA balls. Other leagues use a variety of colors as well as multicolored basketballs.

Just two of the original NBA teams still exist today—the Boston Celtics and the New York Knicks. Every other original team has either folded or moved since the league started.

"Hockey is a sport for white men. Basketball is a sport for black men. Golf is a sport for white men dressed like black pimps."

TIGER WOODS professional golfer

> "If I weren't earning $3 million a year to dunk a basketball, most people on the street would run in the other direction if they saw me coming."

CHARLES BARKLEY
Former NBA pro turned TV pundit

LEATHER FOR CHOICE

Early basketballs were made from four panels of leather stitched together with a rubber bladder inside. A cloth lining was added to the leather for support and uniformity, and, unlike modern balls, they had lacing. This was eventually abandoned in 1937, by which time basketball had become an Olympic sport, having been introduced the previous year in Berlin.

In 1970 the NBA adopted eight rather than four-panel balls as the official ball, while in 1972 Spalding produced the first synthetic leather ball. But in 1983, the company's full-grain leather ball became the NBA's new official ball.

A PEACH OF AN IDEA

Despite being as American as apple pie, basketball was, in fact, invented by a Canadian, James Naismith, in 1891. Naismith was in charge of physical education at Springfield College, Massachusetts, and was looking for an indoor sport to play during the cold winter months.

Naismith's first version involved lobbing a soccer ball into an old peach basket. By 1893 peach baskets had been replaced by iron hoops and hammock-style baskets so that the referee didn't have to climb a ladder and remove the ball after every score.

The change to the basket wasn't the only amendment to Naismith's original rules. The first draft stated that there were nine players on each team and a "player cannot run with the ball" and "must throw it from the spot on which he catches it." In 2010, the first copy of the rules was bought by philanthropist David Booth for $4,338,500.

In 1894, at Naismith's behest, the first purpose-made basketballs were developed by the Spalding Sporting Goods Company. Spalding benefitted enormously from being there at the start, because when the official rules of the game were drawn up, they contained the phrase "… the ball made by A.G. Spalding & Bros. shall be the official ball," which holds to this day.

BOUNCY, BOUNCY

In the nineties,
basketballs with a textured
pebble surface were introduced.
These gave better contact between
the player's finger pads and the
ball, so that passing and shooting
became more accurate, as well
as making it easier to
impart spin to
the ball.

Today, a standard 29½in (75cm) basketball has
about 4,118 "pebbles" on its outer surface,
and the pebbles have a diameter of a tenth
of an inch (2.5mm).

Another major innovation came in 2001, when
Spalding produced the Infusion ball, which had
a built-in pump; and then in 2005 came the Never
Flat, which the company guaranteed would
have a consistent bounce for at least a year.

Not all innovations have been well received, however. In January 2006, the NBA introduced yet another new official ball, Spalding's Cross Traxxion, but players claimed that it was slippery, hard to hold, and the ball's increased friction cut their hands. In addition, the new ball bounced an average of 4in (10cm) less than the old leather ball, as well as absorbing moisture more slowly.

Cross Traxxion lasted just one season before the NBA went back to a traditional leather ball. The current Spalding Official Game NBA Basketball has a top-grade, full-grain Horween leather cover and retails for $169.99. And it's orange …

HE SHOOTS, HE SCORES

The record for the longest basketball shot is 415ft (126.5m). The feat, by YouTubers How Ridiculous, was achieved by throwing the ball from the side of Australia's Gordon Dam into a net positioned on the ground below.

On November 12, 2015, players from the Harlem Globetrotters broke three world records for throwing a basketball into the hoop. Firstly, Thunder Law broke the record for a blindfolded shot by sinking a 69-ft, 6-in (21.2-m) jumper. Next, Handles Franklin nailed a 60-ft, 7-in (18.5-m) throw to break the record for the furthest shot while kneeling down. Finally, Big Easy Lofton hit a 50-ft, 3-in (15.3-m) basket to claim the record for the longest hook shot.

CURRENT BALLS

Leather remains one of the main materials of choice for the outer panels, although the molded rubber composite basketball was introduced in 1942. This had the advantages of being cheaper to produce and less prone to wear and tear, especially when used on rough outdoor surfaces.

Balls are generally designated for either indoor or all-surface use. Indoor-use balls are made of leather or absorbent composites and all-surface ones, known as indoor/outdoor balls, are made of rubber or durable composites.

Major basketball manufacturers besides Spalding include Rawlings, who have produced basketballs since 1902 and make a 10-panel ball known as the TEN; Wilson, who produce the official NCAA game ball; and Molten, a Japanese company who provide the International Basketball Federation (FIBA) and the Olympic Games with their official balls.

Indoor balls are generally more expensive than all-surface ones, and may have to be broken in first to scuff up the surface for better grip when in play.

3

CRICKET

> "Cricket civilizes people and creates good gentlemen."

ROBERT MUGABE President of Zimbabwe

ODD BALLS

The characteristics of a cricket ball change during the game. Fast bowlers prefer to play with a new ball since it is harder, travels faster, and bounces more than an older one. Older balls are better for spin bowlers because their rougher surface imparts better spin.

Ball tampering can give bowlers an unfair advantage against batsmen. As a result, the rules of the game instruct that it's forbidden to:

- Rub any substance apart from saliva or sweat onto the ball
- Rub the ball on the ground
- Scuff the ball with any rough object, including fingernails
- Pick at or lift the seam of the ball

Rain stopping play is a common occurrence in cricket, but on rare occasions the animal kingdom likes to throw a spanner in the works, too. In the past, a pig, sparrow, hedgehog, mouse, and a swarm of bees have all managed to halt progress on the pitch.

Shoaib Akhtar of Pakistan, also known as the "Rawalpindi Express," is regarded as the fastest bowler in the history of cricket. He set a world record with a delivery of 100.2 mph (161.3 km/h) against England in the 2003 World Cup.

How bowling speeds in cricket are classified:		
	mph	km/h
Fast (express)	90+	145+
Fast-medium	80–89	129–145
Medium-fast	70–79	113–129
Medium	60–69	97–113
Medium-slow	50–59	80–97
Slow-medium	40–49	64–80
Slow	below 40	below 64

The Hot Spot is an infrared imaging system that allows the umpire to determine where the ball has struck—the infrared image shows a bright spot where contact friction from the ball has elevated the local temperature. Two cameras positioned at either end of the ground measure heat friction generated by the impact of ball on pad, bat, glove, and anywhere else.

Edward "Lumpy" Stevens of Chertsey and, later, Surrey was one of the first bowlers to use the overarm delivery effectively.

Ball Spin RPM now features on TV to show the rotation speed of the ball when spin bowlers are in action, or how fast the ball is spinning after release.

PUT A CORK IN IT

The essential ingredients of a modern cricket ball are very utilitarian—a cork core layered with tightly wound string and covered by a leather case.

Early cricket balls were basic. A lump of wood was used in an eighth-century Punjab bat-and-ball game called *gilli-danda*, and a game that involved throwing stones or sheep dung at an opponent, using a tree trunk as a wicket, was played in England after the Norman invasion of 1066.

By the seventeenth century things were more high-tech. Balls were made from leather stuffed with cloth, hair, and feathers, or a mix of cork and wool known as a "quilt." These were made by "quiltwinders" who wound a length of thread around an octagonal piece of cork to make a core for the leather-bound ball.

The first official regulations for the ball's dimensions date back to 1774, the same time that faster overarm bowling began to replace underarm bowling. The introduction of a standard size and weight for the ball helped the batsmen and the bowlers since it made the delivery more predictable.

A few years before this, the Duke family from the Eden Valley in Kent started manufacturing the first six-seamed cricket ball, a forerunner of those used in the game today.

The cork core used in balls gave hardness and bounce at the same time as providing enough give to ensure that wooden cricket bats were not damaged. The stitching around the ball was squashed into a spherical shape with a tool called, yes, a "squeezer."

Duke cricket balls are said to keep their shine longer than other balls. The Duke Special County "A" Grade 1 red cricket ball is used exclusively for Test matches in the UK and first-class county cricket, while the Duke County International "A" is the choice of most ECB (England and Wales Cricket Board) accredited Premier League games.

HIGH-TECH BALLS

Australian company Kookaburra was established in 1890 by Alfred Grace Thompson. By 1946 the company was machine-manufacturing balls at a custom-built plant in Melbourne and later developed state-of-the-art machines for cricket-ball production.

Alfred Reader & Company is one of the UK's largest manufacturers of cricket balls. In the 1970s Reader was using high-tech research and development to produce balls made from synthetic cork. The company worked in partnership with Tiflex Limited from Liskeard in Cornwall, which specializes in research into impact abrasion and vibration-absorbing compounds.

RED OR WHITE?

The outside of a modern cricket ball is made from four separate pieces of leather. Two pairs are sewn together on the inside, forming two halves, and the join in one half is rotated at 90 degrees to the other. A raised seam between these two halves is sewn together with six rows of stitches made from string. The ball is then usually dyed red, but other colored balls, such as orange or yellow, are used for improved visibility, along with white for floodlit matches.

The origin of the traditional deep-red color of cricket balls is disputed, although one explanation is that it may have derived from the pigment reddle (red ocher), which was used to brand sheep.

White balls swing more and deteriorate faster than red balls—the polyurethane coating added to a white ball to prevent it getting dirty is the reason for the extra swing. Some claim that white balls are harder than red ones, hurt fielders' hands, and can even break bats.

"You might not think that's cricket, and it's not, it's motor racing."

MURRAY WALKER motorsport commentator and journalist

4

FOOTBALL/ SOCCER

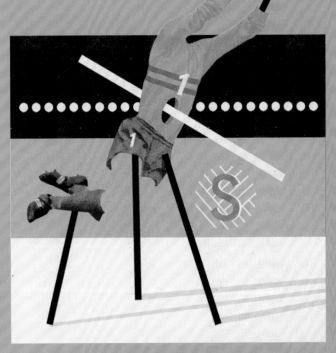

> "Some people believe football is a matter of life and death. I am very disappointed with that attitude ... It is much, much more important than that."

BILL SHANKLY

former professional player and manager of Liverpool FC

ODD BALLS

In 1979 a Scottish Cup tie between Falkirk and Inverness Thistle was postponed 29 times because of bad weather.

The Isles of Scilly have two football teams, the Gunners and the Wanderers. They play each other every week in the league, and also meet in cup ties.

The Albanian national team left the UK in disgrace in 1990 after a stopover at Heathrow, where they went on a literal free-for-all in the airport shops, believing that "duty free" meant "help yourself."

Pedro Gatica cycled from Argentina to Mexico for the 1986 World Cup, but couldn't afford to get into the matches, so he set about haggling for a ticket. While doing so his bike was stolen.

Romanian midfielder Ion Radu was sold by second division Jiul Petrosani to Valcea in 1998 for 1,102lb (500kg) of pork.

DODGY DECISIONS

A Brazilian referee left the match where
he'd been officiating on horseback at
a swift gallop after shooting dead a player
who disputed a penalty decision.

Danish referee Henning Erikstrup was officiating
at the Norager versus Ebeltoft league match when,
as he was about to blow for full-time, his dentures
fell out. While he was searching for them, Ebeltoft
leveled the score to 4–4, but despite their protests,
Erikstrup disallowed the goal, popped his teeth
back in, and blew the final whistle.

**When the Football Association was set up in
1863, there was much discussion over Rule X:
"... any player ... shall be at liberty to charge,
hold, trip or hack [his opponents]." It was
subsequently dropped.**

KEEP UP

The world keepie-uppie record is held by Dan
Magness of England, who kept a regulation football in
the air for 26 hours using just his feet, legs, shoulders,
and head. He is also the holder of the record for the
longest distance traveled while doing keepie-uppie,
managing to go 36 miles (48km) without letting the
ball touch the ground, and in the process visiting
five Premier League grounds in London.

Milene Domingues (a model and former women's footballer, also the ex-wife of striker Ronaldo) holds the record for the longest keepie-uppie if measured by the number of touches accumulated—55,198.

"LOSER DIES"

In South America 3,000 years ago, the Mayans played a form of football using a solid rubber ball that weighed up to 20lb (9kg) and was 20in (50cm) wide. The losers were often sacrificed to the gods. The Aztecs played a similar "loser dies" game called *tlachtli*.

China's Han Dynasty (206 BC–220 AD) had a game called *tsu chu* (*tsu*, "kicking the ball with feet"; *chu*, "a stuffed ball made of leather") and the Japanese played a football-style game called *kemari* around 2,000 years ago.

In North America, Native Americans were recorded in the early seventeenth century playing a violent game of 500-a-side football called *pasuckuakohowog*.

The Aboriginal people of Australia's modern-day Victoria played a version of football called *marn grook*, while in the Middle Ages Italy had *calcio* and France *soule* or *choule*, both using a stitched leather ball stuffed with leather and bran and deriving from a Roman game called *harpastum*.

HIDE YOUR CHILDREN

Football of sorts has been played in England from the eighth century onward. Games were often played between neighboring towns and villages with hundreds of players kicking nine bells out of each other as well as the ball, which was an inflated pig's bladder encased in leather.

Modern-day examples can be seen in Christmas and Hogmanay games at Kirkwall in the Orkneys and Duns in Berwickshire, and Shrove Tuesday matches at Alnwick, Corfe Castle, and Sedgefield. Shop windows may be boarded up to prevent them being smashed in the melee, and children and small dogs are ushered indoors to safety.

MAKING A BALL OF IT

In 1855 Charles Goodyear designed the first footballs to be made with vulcanized rubber bladders. Prior to this, balls made from pig's bladders were standard.

The ball consisted of 18 sections arranged in six panels of three strips each, with a lace-up slit on one side. The ball case was stitched inside out and then reversed so the stitching was on the inside. A bladder was inserted and inflated through one remaining slit, which was then laced up.

The Football Association officially codified the rules of the game and, in 1872, decided on the weight and dimensions of the ball. To all intents and purposes, these are still in use today in world football.

During the early twentieth century, it was common for footballs to deflate during the course of a match.

The old brown leather balls would soak up moisture and gain considerable weight, and this along with the protruding lacing often resulted in head and neck injuries. As late as the 1970s, West Brom player Jeff Astle and Danny Blanchflower of Spurs both suffered chronic brain injuries as a result of heading heavy footballs, which eventually led to their deaths.

Later, various synthetics were applied to the ball's outer casing to repel water, and a new valve was introduced, which did away with the need to have a laced slit on the ball.

In the 1940s a cloth carcass was inserted between the outer and the bladder to maintain the shape of the ball, as well as providing a certain amount of dampening and additional strength.

White balls were introduced in the 1950s as they were easier to see under floodlights, and orange balls for snowy conditions.

PANEL GAMES

In the 1950s Danish company Select developed the 32-panel ball, which maintained a more spherical shape than the 18-panel version.

Black-and-white footballs were introduced for the 1970 Mexico World Cup, because they were easier to see on TV. The iconic Adidas Telstar ball had 12 black pentagons and 20 white hexagons.

For the 2018 World Cup, Adidas reimagined the Telstar and fitted it with an NFC (near field communication) chip that transmits data and allows fans to interact with the ball via an app.

The Nike Ordem V ball is used by the Premier League, Serie A, and La Liga. It has a fuse-welded synthetic leather casing and a geometric 12-panel design, plus Aerowtrac grooves, which provide an accurate and stable flight.

FOR THE LOVE OF THE GAME?

According to *Forbes* magazine, Christiano Ronaldo is the world's highest-earning footballer, taking home a cool $93 million in 2017.

At the opposite end of the pay scale is Kevin Poole. In 2013, English club Burton Albion suffered an injury crisis that left them without a reserve goalkeeper. Luckily, Poole, one of the club coaches, was a former goalkeeper. He agreed to sit on the bench provided Burton Albion paid him with cookies, specifically chocolate Hobnobs.

LONG-RANGE EFFORTS

The world record for the longest goal scored in a professional football match is held by Stoke City goalkeeper Asmir Begović. 13 seconds after kick off against Southampton, Begović cleared a back pass from his defender, hoofing the ball 100 yards, past Southampton's keeper Artur Boruc and into the net.

The fastest goal scored in a game is two seconds, when Nawaf Al Abed took a shot after being passed the ball from the kick off. It was the first goal in a 4–0 victory for Al-Hilal against Al-Shoalah in the Saudi league.

RESPECT YOUR ELDERS

At the time of writing, the oldest active pro footballer is 50-year-old Kazuyoshi Miura, a forward for Yokohama FC in Japan's J-League.

Neil McBain is the oldest player in English Football League history. His career spanned 33 years and seven clubs before retirement in 1947 at the age of 51.

The oldest player to play in a professional game is Salvador Reyes. In 2008, the 71-year-old Reyes kicked off a game for his old club, CD Guadalajara, before being substituted. The youngest ever player in a professional match was Mauricio Baldevieso, who in 2009, at the age of 12 years, 362 days, played as a striker for Bolivian side Aurora.

Scouting youth talent is a key part of the game, but Belgian club FC Racing Boxberg took things to extremes by signing Bryce Brites, a 20-month-old baby.

GOLF

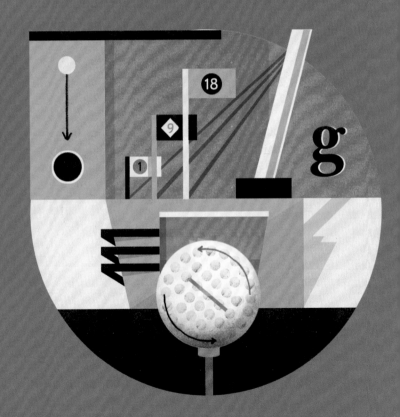

"If you are caught on a golf course during a storm and are afraid of lightning, hold up a 1-iron. Not even God can hit a 1-iron."

LEE TREVINO former professional golfer, who was struck by lightning while playing in the Western Open in Chicago in 1975

ODD BALLS

While playing a round in 1899, American Ab Smith produced what he described as a "bird of a shot," and the term "birdie" evolved from there.

The longest recorded drive on an ordinary golf course is 515 yards by Michael Hoke Austin of Los Angeles, California, in the US National Seniors Open Championship at Las Vegas, Nevada on September 25, 1974.

A putt measured at 140ft 2¾in was sunk on the 18th hole at St Andrews by Bob Cook in the International Fourball Pro Am Tournament on October 1, 1976.

Pro golfer John Hudson scored two consecutive holes-in-one at the 11th and 12th holes (195 yards and 311 yards respectively) in the 1971 Martini Tournament at Norwich, England. The chance of this is 67,000,000:1.

Annual worldwide production of golf balls: 850 million.

The longest hole-in-one is 427 yards at the 16th at Lake Hefner course, Oklahoma City, USA by Lou Kretlow in March 1961.

"What most people don't understand is that UFOs are on a cosmic tourist route. That's why they're always seen in Arizona, Scotland, and New Mexico. Another thing to consider is that all three of those destinations are good places to play golf. So there's possibly some connection between aliens and golf."

ALICE COOPER
singer-songwriter whose brand of hard rock is designed to shock

HAMMERS AND FEATHERS

The first golf balls were made from wood and were used in Scotland in 1550, although there are records of games similar to golf being played in China in the eleventh century and Holland in the thirteenth century.

A ball known as the "featherie" was introduced in Scotland in 1618, so called because it was made from a leather case packed with a "top hat full" of boiled goose or chicken feathers.

The materials were wet during construction so that as they dried out the feathers expanded and the leather contracted. The ball was hammered into a round shape, coated with several layers of paint, and punched with the ball maker's mark to create a hard ball that could be driven hundreds of yards.

80 percent of all golfers will never achieve a handicap of less than 18.

The longest recorded drive of a featherie was 361 yards by Samuel Messieux in 1836 on St Andrews Old Course, although a typical drive was 150–175 yards (compared with 180–250 yards with a modern ball).

Featheries were expensive, as were clubs, so golf was a rich man's sport.

PUT YOUR GUT INTO IT

In 1848 Rev. Dr Robert Adams Paterson of St Andrews introduced the "guttie" ball, which was less expensive than the featherie and could be repaired. It brought more people into the game.

The guttie was made by boiling *gutta-percha*, a rubbery tree sap, until it became soft and could be hand-rolled on a board into the correct size and shape.

A renowned maker of gutties was Allan Robertson of St Andrews, one of the first pro golfers. In 1859 he became the first person to record a round of under 80 on the Old Course at St Andrews.

Gutties with a rough surface were found to have a truer flight and travel farther than other versions, which led to balls being beaten with a sharp-edged hammer. By the 1880s gutties were made in molds that created patterns on the surface—forerunners of the dimpled golf ball.

Rubber companies, such as Dunlop, began to mass-produce golf balls, which pretty much resulted in the end of hand-crafted balls.

HASKELL'S BALL

In 1898 US golfer Coburn Haskell came up with the next major development in golf balls, the rubber-core ball. Produced by rubber company B.F. Goodrich (later famous for their tires), these balls were made from a solid rubber core wrapped in rubber thread and encased in a gutta-percha outer casing. They gave the average golfer a good 20 yards extra length in driving from the tee.

In short order, the rubber-core golf ball went into mass production. In the early 1900s, gutta-percha balls were replaced with balata and in 1905 dimpled golf balls made their first appearance.

KING OF THE SWINGERS

The average speed of a PGA pro's swing is around 113 mph, which should send the ball a little under 300 yards. One of the game's biggest swingers is Bubba Watson. In 2015, his average swing speed was 123.52 mph and average drive distance was 315.2 yards. Compare this with one of the slowest swingers, Ben Crane, who has an average clubhead speed of 104.59 mph and drive distance of 271 yards.

DRAG ARTIST

Dimpled balls travel farther than smooth balls as a result of the turbulence caused by the dimples, which reduces drag.

The size and number of the dimples affects the ball's aerodynamics. There are no rules for how many dimples a ball can have—392 is the average and most have between 300 and 500.

Maximum velocity of a golf ball:
250ft per second.

The more dimples, the better the ball's stability in flight, but there's a trade-off. The more dimples, the less space between them, and if this is too narrow, it may shear on impact with either the club or the ground and the ball will scuff.

Most dimples ever on a golf ball: 1,070.

A wide variation in ball sizes and weights existed when dimpled balls were introduced, and surprisingly it was not until 1991 that standard dimensions for golf balls were agreed between the two main golfing authorities, the Royal & Ancient in Scotland and the United States Golf Association in the USA.

> "I have a tip that will take five strokes off anyone's golf game. It's called an eraser."

ARNOLD PALMER former professional golfer

EXPLODING BALLS

B.F. Goodrich returned to the scene in 1906 with a pneumatic golf ball (known to explode in hot conditions), followed by experiments with cores of cork, mercury, and metal among other substances. However, the rubber-core golf ball remained the most popular until Spalding brought out the two-piece Executive ball in the 1970s.

Today there are essentially four different types of golf ball:

- One piece: basic, inexpensive balls made from a solid piece of Surlyn thermoplastic with molded dimples

- Two piece: hard-wearing balls suitable for long driving and popular with recreational golfers. Made with a solid, hard-plastic core of high-energy acrylate or resin covered with tough Surlyn or specialty plastic

- Three piece: made with a core that either contains a gel or liquid (such as sugar and water) or is solid, windings of rubber thread, and a plastic cover

- Four piece: made with a solid rubber core, two inner covers, and a thin but durable urethane outer layer to provide a longer hit and a better feel on the green

6

RUGBY

"I couldn't very well
hit him could I? I had
the ball in my hands."

TOMMY BISHOP former rugby league player and coach,
when questioned about kicking a fellow player

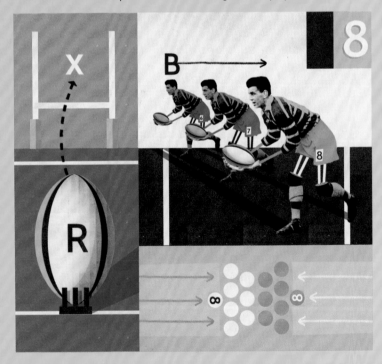

ODD BALLS

The first international rugby union match was between Scotland and England in 1871 at Raeburn Park in Edinburgh. Scotland won 1–0 after William Cross converted a try. Using the present-day scoring system, Scotland would have won 12–5 as they scored two tries and one conversion against England's one try, which they failed to convert.

The reigning Olympic rugby champions are the United States. Rugby Union featured in the Olympics in 1900, 1908, 1920, and 1924. The USA won on the last two occasions and consequently are the most successful Olympic rugby team.

Western Samoa's first international was against Fiji in 1924—there was a tree in the middle of the pitch and the game kicked off at 7 a.m. so the Samoans could go to work afterward.

"Rugby is a game for the mentally deficient ... That is why it was invented by the British. Who else but an Englishman could invent an oval ball?"

PETER COOK English comedian, actor, satirist, and writer

In 2007, an Australian rugby player complained of headaches and lethargy for some weeks after a game. A couple of months later, when he suffered a head injury that required examination, it was discovered he'd had another player's tooth embedded in his skull for all that time ...

The first national anthem sung at a rugby international was on November 16, 1905 when Wales played New Zealand at Cardiff Arms Park. After New Zealand performed the Haka (the Maori's ancestral war dance), the Welsh team responded with *Hen Wlad Fy Nhadau*, and the crowd joined in.

Morley RUFC (rugby union football club) remains a bastion of unionism in Yorkshire, the heartland of rugby league, as a result of the club's two representatives missing the 1895 meeting in Huddersfield, at which the split from union was organized. They decided to stop off for "a drink or two" *en route* to the meeting and consequently missed their train.

A try was so named because it gave the player who scored one the opportunity to try to score a goal by kicking the ball between two posts and over the crossbar, thus converting the try to a goal. The try itself actually earned no points at all.

The Gil Evans whistle is used to start the opening game of every Rugby Union World Cup. It was first used by Welsh referee Gil Evans in the match between England and New Zealand in 1905, and it was also used at the kick-off of the final of the 1924 Paris Olympics.

RUNNING WITH THE BALL

The invention of rugby is credited to William Webb Ellis of Rugby School in Warwickshire in 1823. A form of football in which the hands were used had been played at the school since 1750, but Webb Ellis took it further. He was accused of cheating, and consequently "held in low regard."

In the Roman game of *harpastum* both hands and feet were used, and games such as "cnapan" in Pembrokeshire, Wales, "campball" in eastern England, "hurling to goales" in Cornwall, southwest England, and the "Atherstone Ball Game", Warwickshire, all date from medieval times and have similarities to modern-day rugby.

By 1845, Rugby School had developed rules for the game—prior to this, 300 or more players would take part in a school match—and the first balls made specifically for the sport were constructed in 1832 by William Gilbert (1799–1877). He was shoemaker to Rugby School and, in 1842, moved to premises directly opposite the school's playing field.

INFLATED BLADDERS

Early games used a bladder filled with paper or straw and no two balls were ever the same shape, size, or weight. Later balls were made from four pieces of cowhide stitched together and inflated by a pig's bladder, which gave the "prolate sphere" shape. The bladder, still green and smelly, was inflated through the stem of a clay pipe.

According to E.F.T. Bennett, who played for Rugby School in the mid-1800s, "The shape of our ball came from the bladder and was a perfect ball for long drop kicking or placing and for dribbling too ..."

In 1870, Richard Lindop, a former pupil at Rugby School, invented an inflatable rubber bladder, which was both easier to blow up and helped prevent illnesses caused through inflating a raw pig's bladder by lung power.

In the late nineteenth century, a ball inflator was invented, based on an enlarged ear syringe.

In 1871 William Gilbert's nephew James Gilbert exhibited the Rugby School Football at the Great Exhibition in London under "Educational Appliances" and went on to export rugby balls to British colonies, including Australia, New Zealand, and South Africa.

BALL INNOVATIONS

The Rugby Football Union (RFU) was founded in 1871, and in 1892 it introduced standard dimensions for the ball. Four panels became the official construction technique. Prior to this six and eight-panel balls were also produced.

Materials for the ball's outer covering included camel hide and pigskin as well as cowhide. The first two were easier to work with but were not popular with players since they were slippery when wet.

Henry Timms, who made some 50,000 balls for Gilbert between 1890 and 1935, introduced the technique of dry-leather stitching. Balls no longer had to be made up wet and dried out before being dispatched to market.

TWO CAN PLAY AT THAT GAME

In 1895, rugby split into two codes, union and league. This came about mainly as a result of the RFU enforcing amateurism on the game— a harsh imposition on the working-class northern clubs, whose players relied heavily on "broken-time payments" in order to take time off work to play the game.

There is very little difference between the balls used by union and league. Rugby League balls are a bit smaller and traditionally have six panels as this gives a more pointy shape, which is better for kicking, although today four-panel balls are increasingly common. The balls may be similar but to quote Tony Collins, professor of the social history of sport at Leeds Metropolitan University, "The only thing the two sports really have in common is the shape of the posts and the balls."

NEW BALLS

The dimensions of the union ball were reduced by an inch (2.5cm) and the weight raised by 1.45oz (41g) in 1932 to make it better for handling, although different nations had their own design preferences. The Kiwis and Aussies preferred torpedo-shaped balls, South Africans went for eight panels for better grip, and the UK nations stayed with four panels.

Gilbert remained the main manufacturer for both union and league balls up to the 1970s. Gilbert Match, made from cowhide, was the standard issue for union internationals in 1960. For a while, Gilbert remained with natural leather as other companies moved on to various synthetics and laminates that reduced water retention and allowed better handling.

Companies such as Webb Ellis, and in rugby league, Steeden from Australia, are the other major players in the market today.

Gilbert still provides the official Rugby Union World Cup ball in the form of the Gilbert Match XV, a synthetic and laminate structure, which uses a patented Multi-Matrix pimple pattern for better handling. Star-shaped and round pimples had been used before this, again on synthetic rather than leather surfaces.

In Australia, Steeden's name is often used generically for a rugby league ball.

A modern rugby ball from either code is a complex composite of modern materials technology, using computational fluid dynamics analysis, nanotechnology, and 3D modeling to determine the optimum shape and placement of the pimples for minimum drag and maximum travel. All a far cry from a straw-filled bladder ...

HIGH SCORES

The highest scoring game in the Rugby Union World Cup was when New Zealand beat Japan 145–17 on June 4, 1995.

The highest score in an international rugby league match is France's 120–0 defeat of Serbia and Montenegro in the Mediterranean Cup played in Beirut, Lebanon on October 22, 2003.

The highest score ever was recorded on February 8, 2015 in Belgium when Royal Kituro beat Soignies 356–3. Kituro ran in 56 tries, meaning they crossed the line roughly every 90 seconds.

7

TENNIS

> "Tennis is a perfect combination of violent action taking place in an atmosphere of total tranquility."

BILLIE JEAN KING former world number one, founder of the Women's Tennis Association, World Team Tennis, and the Women's Sports Foundation

ODD BALLS

A tennis ball's coefficient of drag is calculated thus: Co = D/0.5 q u² A where D is the drag force, q is the density of air (1.21 kg/m²), u is the velocity of the ball relative to the fluid, and A the cross-sectional area.

The fuzzy surface of the felt is a vital component in how tennis balls travel through the air. It enables players to impart spin to the ball, since it creates air drag and friction, which allows backspin and topspin. Scientific papers have been written on the subject, and the ITF (International Tennis Federation) have tested tennis balls in wind tunnels and have a special rig designed to test ball spin with different rackets. Even NASA has studied the aerodynamics of tennis balls.

"I love Wimbledon. But why don't they stage it in the summer?"

VIJAY AMRITRAJ former tennis professional discussing the sodden 2007 Wimbledon Championships

Two possible origins of the word "tennis":

- From the French *tenez*, which means "take it/take that." This may have been shouted upon serving the ball in early games.

- From the game's possible—but very speculative—origins in Tinnis, an Egyptian town on the banks of the Nile.

The service was apparently invented by Henry VIII, who had servants throw the ball up for him to strike as he was too fat to do it himself.

The longest match on record took place in 2010 at Wimbledon, when John Isner (USA) and Nicolas Mahut (France) played for 11 hours 5 minutes over three days in a game that Isner eventually won 6–4, 3–6, 6–7 (7), 7–6 (3), 70–68.

The shortest match on record is the 1922 Wimbledon final, where Suzanne Lenglen beat Molla Mallory in 23 minutes.

The use of "love" for zero is shrouded in mystery. One origin is said to be from the French word *l'oeuf* as in "egg," meaning zero.

The official world record speed for a tennis serve is held by Samuel Groth of Australia—163.4 mph (263 km/h) at the Busan Open 2012 Challenger Event. However, there is evidence (though often disputed) that Big Bill Tilden (USA) clocked up 163.6 mph (263.3 km/h) way back in 1931.

The tennis grounds at Wimbledon are owned by All England Lawn Tennis Ground plc and consist of 19 grass courts (including Center Court and No.1 Court), eight American Clay courts, and five indoor courts (two Greenset Velvelux and three Greenset Trophy).

ECCLESIASTICAL TO REGAL PURSUIT

The first accounts of a game approximating to modern tennis originate in eleventh-century France, where monks knocked a crudely fashioned ball back and forth by hand over a rope stretched across a monastery quadrangle.

It was known as *jeu de paume*, due to the use of the palms. Around the twelfth century leather gloves were introduced, then in the sixteenth century short rackets—probably due to the fact that early tennis balls were made from leather stuffed with wool or horsehair and were hard on the palm of the hand.

By this time, the game had evolved into an indoor game, popular among French and British royalty and aristocracy, hence the term "court" for the playing area. This version of the game is still played and is known as Real or Court Tennis.

By the eighteenth century, the ball was made from thin strips of wool wound tightly around an inner core, which was then tied up with string. The whole lot was stitched inside a white cloth outer layer.

Major Walter Clopton Wingfield brought out two books on tennis, *The Book of the Game* (1873) and *The Major's Game of Lawn Tennis* (1874).

TENNIS MOVES OUTSIDE

Tennis as we know it today took off in Victorian times. In 1872 the world's first tennis club was formed in Leamington Spa, based on a game devised by Major Harry Gem and Augurio Pereira, while the following year Major Walter Clopton Wingfield brought out a very similar game called *sphairistike* (from the Greek σφάίρίστική, meaning "skill at playing at ball") or lawn tennis. This was based on the old game played by royalty and used much of the French terminology of the original sport.

> "To be a tennis champion, you have to be inflexible. You have to be stubborn. You have to be arrogant. You have to be selfish and self-absorbed."

CHRIS EVERT former world number one and president of the Women's Tennis Association

At the first Wimbledon Championships, held in 1877, the balls consisted of solid India rubber spheres, although it was soon found that they lasted longer and were better to play with if flannel was stitched on top of the rubber.

The flannel was eventually replaced by hard-wearing Melton cloth, a tight-woven woollen cloth that originated in Melton Mowbray in Leicestershire. This felt fabric is still used today, along with Needle cloth, which is less hard-wearing.

According to the official Wimbledon website, 54,250 balls are used during the Championship. Around 20,000 are allocated for practice purposes and the rest are used on court. During a match, an umpire will request that all balls are changed after seven games are played and then after every nine games.

FEEL THE PRESSURE

Eventually, a hollow rubber sphere was introduced, which was cut to shape using "clover leaf" segments. The ball was filled with pressurizing gases, which were activated as the core was molded by heat into a spherical shape.

Later balls have two separate rubber hemispheres joined together under pressure to give a uniform shape and predictable response.

The felt fabric used on a modern tennis ball is woven using cotton and a wool/nylon mix, after which it's dyed and finished. Then two "dogbones" of fabric are cut, after application of a latex backing, and stuck to the latex-covered core. The ball is cured and tumbled slowly through a steam-laden atmosphere, which causes the cloth to fluff, giving a soft, raised surface. The ridge where the two halves of the ball are cemented together disappears.

The seam on a tennis ball is actually the glue that has come up through the two pieces of felt that make up the surface of the ball.

Logos are applied before the balls are packed in pressurized cans. Balls lose their pressure about a month after opening the can. However, not all tennis balls are pressurized—you can buy pressureless balls with a solid core. These are used mainly for training. They don't lose their bounce as pressurized balls do, although the felt will wear off eventually.

PLENTY OF CHOICE

The ITF introduced yellow balls in 1972 (Wimbledon held off until 1986) because they are easier for TV viewers to see. Up until then tennis balls were white, or occasionally black, depending on the background color of the court.

Just one type of tennis ball was used in competition play until 1989 when high-altitude balls were introduced to allow for different atmospheric pressure. Then in 2002, Types 1, 2, and 3 balls became available—Type 1 for slower courts, 2 for standard courts, and 3 for fast courts.

Tennis balls vary slightly, depending on the manufacturer and model, and experienced players can instantly tell the difference between balls— they may feel lighter or heavier, harder or softer, more or less bouncy, have a coarser or finer cover, and require varying degrees of effort in order to generate the same speed.

8 BASEBALL

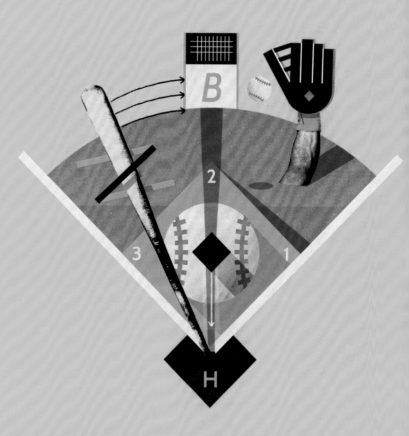

> "Baseball, it is said,
> is only a game. True.
> And the Grand Canyon is
> only a hole in Arizona.
> Not all holes, or games,
> are created equal."

GEORGE WILL US newspaper columnist

ODD BALLS

Before World War Two, baseball enjoyed some popularity in the UK. Many English football/ soccer teams shared their grounds with baseball teams, which is why Derby County's former home was known as the Baseball Ground. In 1938, the Great Britain national team even managed to defeat the United States in the Amateur World Series.

John Smoltz, a pitcher for the Atlanta Braves, burned his chest in 1990 while ironing a shirt that he was wearing.

All Major League Baseball (MLB) umpires must wear black underwear in case their pants split.

A curve ball can curve up to 17½in (44.5cm) in the course of being pitched, travels at between 70 and 80 mph (110 and 130 km/h), and rotates at 1900rpm.

Baseball is closely related to the English schoolgirls' game of rounders—at least according to an article written in 1905 by US sports journalist and Baseball Hall of Famer Henry Chadwick, although some aspects, such as the box score, are derived directly from cricket.

SPALDING'S CALL

From 1871 to 1875, A.G. Spalding, the 'inventor' of the baseball as we know it today, pitched every game with a baseball he had developed himself. He won 241 out of 301 games, went on to be inducted in the Baseball Hall of Fame, and for the next 100 years his baseball was the official ball of the US Major Leagues.

Over his career with Boston Red Stockings and Chicago White Stockings, Spalding achieved a 0.323 batting average, an earned-run average of 2.14, and an overall winning percentage of 0.796, a record that still stands today.

"I can wear a baseball cap; I am entitled to wear a baseball cap. I am genetically pre-disposed to wear a baseball cap, whereas most English people look wrong in a baseball cap."

BILL BRYSON author

> "There are three types of baseball players: Those who make it happen, those who watch it happen, and those who wonder what happens."

TOMMY LASORDA former Major League player

MATERIAL THINGS

According to the website for MLB (Major League Baseball), the ball 'shall be a sphere formed by yarn wound around a small core of cork, rubber, or similar material, covered with two stripes of white horsehide or cowhide, tightly stitched together,' a basic design that has changed remarkably little from the early baseballs invented by A.G. Spalding.

The MBL (Metro Baseball League) balls made today by Rawlings are still made from leather and have raised seams (with a regulation 108 stitches), a design that has been much the same for over 80 years.

"Half this game is 90 percent mental."

DANNY OZARK former Major League coach and manager

DEADBALL

Prior to 1872, when the dimensions and materials for baseballs were established, baseballs were made by hand from a string-wrapped rubber core with a horsehide cover, and varied from golf ball to softball size, and in weight from 3–6oz (85–170g). These early balls were renowned for their "deadball" feel in play, yet this was still a problem when the balls were standardized in 1872. This early period in baseball's history was known as the "Deadball Era" and home runs were a rarity due to the lack of response from the ball when whacked.

In 1910 George Reach of Reach Sporting Goods invented a baseball with a cork center, which was much more responsive. These balls were secretly used in the 1910 World Series (named after the *New York World* newspaper according to some; as a result of American hubris according to others) and with them the number of home runs increased, leading to cork balls becoming the standard for Major League Baseball in 1911.

During World War Two, the US military developed the T-13 Beano hand grenade, which was designed to the same specifications as a baseball. The thinking behind this was that every American man should be familiar with throwing a baseball, therefore encouraging more accurate throwing by soldiers.

"If it wasn't for baseball,
I'd be in either the
penitentiary or the cemetery."

BABE RUTH former Major League player

SMALL CHANGES

Pitchers developed new styles of deliveries to take full advantage of the more responsive ball. "Scuffballs," for instance, involved the pitcher rubbing a smooth spot on the ball, which caused it both to spin and travel more quickly. It's now banned due to the potential danger to the batter.

White balls became more common as they were easier for the batter to see and hit, which led to an increase in the number of runs being scored. To even things out, a 1931 change favored pitchers. A thin layer of rubber was wrapped around the cork core and the seams were raised. These changes deadened the ball slightly and the raised seams allowed pitchers to get a better grip to impart more rotation to the ball.

The number of balls used in a game from the 1920s onward could be between 20 and 60, because it became the fashion for fans to keep foul balls as souvenirs, instead of handing them in for free admission to another game. Also, umpires would remove dirty, worn, or scuffed balls from play much sooner than they had done previously.

No more noticeable changes took place in the design of the ball until Spalding, then the world's major manufacturer of baseballs and official supplier to the MLB, changed from cowhide to horsehide covers in 1974 for economic reasons.

Today the average number of baseballs used per game is 120, with the average life span of a ball being five to seven pitches. The 30 MLB teams get through more than 900,000 balls each season, which costs somewhere in the order of $5.5 million per year (less than the average salary of a New York Yankees player).

"Baseball is very big with my people. It figures. It's the only way we can get to shake a bat at a white man without starting a riot."

DICK GREGORY

African-American comedian, writer, and civil rights activist